Congressional Research Service
Informing the legislative debate since 1914

Reaching the Debt Limit: Background and Potential Effects on Government Operations

Mindy R. Levit, Coordinator
Specialist in Public Finance

Clinton T. Brass
Specialist in Government Organization and Management

Thomas J. Nicola
Legislative Attorney

Dawn Nuschler
Specialist in Income Security

November 21, 2013

Congressional Research Service

7-5700

www.crs.gov

R41633

Summary

The gross federal debt, which represents the federal government's total outstanding debt, consists of (1) debt held by the public and (2) debt held in government accounts, also known as intragovernmental debt. Federal government borrowing increases for two primary reasons: (1) budget deficits and (2) investments of any federal government account surpluses in Treasury securities, as required by law. Nearly all of this debt is subject to the statutory limit. The federal government's statutory debt limit is currently suspended through February 7, 2014.

Treasury has yet to face a situation in which it was unable to pay its obligations as a result of reaching the debt limit. In the past, the debt limit has always been raised before the debt reached the limit. However, on several occasions Treasury took extraordinary actions to avoid reaching the limit which, as a result, affected the operations of certain programs. If the Secretary of the Treasury determines that the issuance of obligations of the United States may not be made without exceeding the public debt limit, Treasury can make use of "extraordinary measures." Some of these measures require the Treasury Secretary to authorize a debt issuance suspension period.

Since 2011, the debt limit has been increased through provisions of three pieces of legislation. The debt limit was increased on August 2, 2011, as part of the Budget Control Act of 2011 (BCA; P.L. 112-25). The BCA also provided for two additional debt limit increases, which occurred in September 2011 and January 2012. On February 4, 2013, the statutory debt limit was suspended through May 18, 2013, as part of the No Budget, No Pay Act of 2013 (P.L. 113-3). On May 19, 2013, the debt limit was reinstated at a level which accommodated borrowing incurred during the suspension period (February 4 to May 18, 2013). On October 17, 2013, the debt limit was suspended again through February 7, 2014, as part of the Continuing Appropriations Act, 2014 (P.L. 113-46). Between the enactment of each of these legislative measures, Treasury used extraordinary measures to continue financing obligations.

Budget outlays and revenue collections along with the funds contained in the extraordinary measures will affect the timing of when the debt limit is reached. If the debt limit is reached and Treasury is no longer able to issue federal debt, federal outlays would have to be decreased or federal revenues would have to be increased by a corresponding amount to cover the gap in what cannot be borrowed.

It is extremely difficult for Congress to effectively influence short-term fiscal and budgetary policy through action on legislation adjusting the debt limit. The need to raise (or lower) the limit during a session of Congress is driven by previous decisions regarding revenues and spending stemming from legislation enacted earlier in the session or in prior years. Nevertheless, the consideration of debt limit legislation often is viewed as an opportunity to reexamine fiscal and budgetary policy. Consequently, House and Senate action on legislation adjusting the debt limit is often complicated, hindered by policy disagreements, and subject to delay.

Contents

Appendixes

Contacts

The federal government's statutory debt limit is currently suspended through February 7, 2014 (P.L. 113-46).[1] Absent further legislative action, the debt limit will be reinstated on February 8, 2014, at a level which will accommodate the borrowing incurred during the suspension period. At that time, Treasury is expected to begin utilizing its authority outside of its typical cash management practices to pay federal obligations to delay the date by which the debt limit would impede the federal government's ability to make timely payments on all of its obligations (through a debt issuance suspension period as well as other methods discussed in more detail later in this report). Similar actions have been taken previously. If these financing options are exhausted and Treasury is no longer able to pay for all federal obligations, some federal payments to creditors, vendors, contractors, state and local governments, beneficiaries, and other entities would be delayed or limited. This could result in significant economic and financial consequences that may have a lasting impact on federal programs and the federal government's ability to borrow in the future.

This report examines the possibility of the federal government reaching its statutory debt limit and not raising it, with a particular focus on government operations. First, the report explains the nature of the federal government's debt, the processes associated with federal borrowing, and historical events that may influence prospective actions. It also includes an analysis of what *could* happen if the federal government may no longer issue debt, has exhausted alternative sources of cash, and, therefore, depends on incoming receipts or other sources of funds to provide any cash needed to liquidate federal obligations.[2] A discussion of the effects that prior debt limit impasses have had on the economy is also included. Finally, this report lays out considerations for increasing the debt limit under current policy and what impact fiscal policy could have on the debt limit going forward.

Federal Government Debt and the Debt Limit[3]

The gross federal debt, which represents the federal government's total outstanding debt, consists of:

- the debt held by the public and

- the debt held in government accounts, also known as intragovernmental debt.

Federal government borrowing increases for two primary reasons: (1) budget deficits and (2) investments of any federal government account surpluses in Treasury securities as required by law.[4]

---

[1] The current level of federal debt can be found in the U.S. Department of the Treasury, *Daily Treasury Statement*, Table III-C, available at http://fms.treas.gov/dts/index.html.

[2] The possible scenario sometimes has been referred to generically as a debt limit crisis. U.S. General Accounting Office (now the Government Accountability Office and hereinafter GAO), *Debt Ceiling: Analysis of Actions During the 2003 Debt Issuance Suspension Periods*, GAO-04-526, May 2004.

[3] This section draws on CRS Report 98-453, *Debt-Limit Legislation in the Congressional Budget Process*, by Bill Heniff Jr., and CRS Report RL31967, *The Debt Limit: History and Recent Increases*, by D. Andrew Austin and Mindy R. Levit.

[4] If the budget is in surplus and intragovernmental debt rises by an amount that is less than the budget surplus, the total debt would not increase. See the later discussion in the section titled "Implications of Future Federal Debt on the Debt Limit."

The debt held by the public represents the total net amount borrowed from the public to cover the federal government's accumulated budget deficits. Annual budget deficits increase the debt held by the public by requiring the federal government to borrow additional funds to fulfill its commitments.

The debt held in government accounts represents the federal debt issued to certain accounts, primarily trust funds, such as those associated with Social Security, Medicare, and Unemployment Compensation. Generally, government account surpluses, which include trust fund surpluses, by law must be invested in special non-marketable federal government securities and thus are held in the form of federal debt.[5] Treasury periodically pays interest on the special securities held in a government account. Interest payments are typically paid in the form of additional special securities issued by Treasury to the trust funds, which also increases the amount of intragovernmental debt and federal debt subject to limit.

When a trust fund invests in U.S. Treasury securities, it effectively lends money to the rest of the government. The loan either reduces what the federal government must borrow from the public if the budget is in deficit, or reduces the amount of publicly held debt if the budget is in surplus. At the same time, the loan increases intragovernmental debt. The revenues exchanged for these securities then go into the General Fund of the Treasury and are indistinguishable from other cash in the General Fund. This cash may be used for any government spending purpose.[6]

Congress created a statutory debt limit in the Second Liberty Bond Act of 1917.[7] This development changed Treasury's borrowing process and assisted Congress in its efforts to exercise its constitutional prerogatives to control the federal government's fiscal outcomes. The debt limit also imposes a form of fiscal accountability that compels Congress and the President to take deliberate action to allow further federal borrowing if necessary.

Almost all of the federal government's borrowing is subject to a statutory limit.[8] From time to time, Congress has considered and adopted legislation to change this limit. Because the statutory limit applies to debt held by the public as well as intragovernmental debt, both budget deficits and government account surpluses may contribute to the federal government reaching the existing debt limit.

The Debt Limit and the Treasury

Treasury's standard methods for financing federal activities can be disrupted when the level of federal debt nears its legal limit. If the limit prevents Treasury from issuing new debt to manage

---

[5] GAO, *Federal Trust and Other Earmarked Funds Answers to Frequently Asked Questions*, GAO-01-199SP, January 2001, pp. 17-18.

[6] For an explanation of how this process works for the Social Security Trust Funds, see the section of the **Appendix** titled "Social Security Trust Fund Cash and Investment Management Practices."

[7] Chapter 56, 40 Stat. 288 (1917). The debt limit is now codified at 31 U.S.C. §3101.

[8] Treasury currently defines "Total Public Debt Subject to Limit" as "the Total Public Debt Outstanding less Unamortized Discount on Treasury Bills and Zero-Coupon Treasury Bonds, old debt issued prior to 1917, and old currency called United States Notes, as well as Debt held by the Federal Financing Bank and Guaranteed Debt." Approximately 0.1% of total federal debt is not subject to the debt limit. For more information, see U.S. Office of Management and Budget (hereinafter OMB), *Budget of the U.S. Government for FY2014, Analytical Perspectives*, Chapter 5 and Table 5-2.

short-term cash flows or to finance an annual deficit, the government may be unable to obtain the cash needed to pay its bills. The limit may also prevent the government from issuing new debt in order to invest the surpluses of designated government accounts, such as federal trust funds. Treasury is caught between two requirements: the law that requires Treasury to pay the government's legal obligations or invest trust fund surpluses, on one hand, and the statutory debt limit which may prevent Treasury from issuing the debt to raise cash to pay obligations or make trust fund investments, on the other.[9]

The level of federal debt changes throughout the year due to fluctuations in revenue and outlays, regardless of whether or not the government has an annual surplus or deficit. Seasonal fluctuations could still require Treasury to sell debt even if the annual level of federal debt subject to limit does not increase (i.e., if the budget were balanced and trust funds were not in surplus). Even on a day-to-day basis, the level of federal debt can vary significantly. For example, Treasury issues large volumes of individual income tax refunds in February and March, because taxpayers expecting refunds tend to file early. On the other hand, Treasury tends to collect more revenue in April because taxpayers making payments tend to file closer to April 15.

Past Treasury Secretaries, when faced with a nearly binding debt ceiling, have used special strategies to handle cash and debt management responsibilities.[10] Since 1985, these measures have included

- suspending sales of nonmarketable debt (savings bonds, state and local government series, and other nonmarketable debt);

- trimming or delaying auctions of marketable securities;

- under-investing or disinvesting certain government funds (Social Security, Government Securities Investment Fund of the Federal Thrift Savings Plan, the Civil Service Retirement and Disability Trust Fund, Postal Service Retiree Health Benefit Fund, Exchange Stabilization Fund);[11] and

- exchanging Treasury securities for non-Treasury securities held by the Federal Financing Bank (FFB).

Under current law, if the Secretary of the Treasury determines that the issuance of obligations of the United States may not be made without exceeding the debt limit, a "debt issuance suspension period" may be determined.[12] This determination gives Treasury the authority to suspend investments in the Civil Service Retirement and Disability Trust Fund, Postal Service Retiree Health Benefit Fund, and the Government Securities Investment Fund (G-Fund) of the Federal

---

[9] *See generally,* 31 U.S.C. §§3321 *et seq.* for the Treasury Secretary's duty to pay obligations. Regarding trust fund investments, see, for example, 42 U.S.C. §401 (Social Security Trust Funds), 5 U.S.C. §8348 (Civil Service Retirement and Disability Trust Fund), and 5 U.S.C. §8909 (Postal Service Retiree Health Benefit Fund).

[10] For example, see out-of-print CRS Report 95-1109, *Authority to Tap Trust Funds and Establish Payment Priorities if the Debt Limit is not Increased,* by Thomas J. Nicola and Morton Rosenberg (available from CRS upon request).

[11] Under-investing or disinvesting certain government funds provides room under the debt limit by freezing or reducing the amount of government debt held in these accounts in order to provide head room for more debt to be issued to the public to facilitate sufficient cash flow to pay obligations or to use receipts that would otherwise be invested in Treasury securities for purposes of paying other obligations.

[12] Congress formally authorized the additional powers to the Treasury Secretary under a "debt issuance suspension period" in the Omnibus Budget Reconciliation Act of 1986 (P.L. 99-509) and Thrift Savings Fund Investment Act of 1987 (P.L. 100-43).

Thrift Savings Plan. In addition, this gives Treasury the authority to prematurely redeem securities held by the Civil Service Retirement and Disability Trust Fund and Postal Service Retiree Health Benefit Fund. Debt issuance suspension periods were previously in effect from November 15, 1995, through January 15, 1997; April 4 through April 16, 2002; May 16 through June 28, 2002; February 20 through May 27, 2003; May 16 through August 2, 2011; December 31, 2012, through February 4, 2013; and May 20, 2013 to October 16, 2013.

Past Treasury Actions to Postpone Reaching the Debt Limit

Treasury has yet to face a situation in which it was unable to pay its obligations as a result of reaching the debt limit. However, during debt limit impasses in 1985, 1995-1996, 2002, 2003, 2011, and 2013, Treasury took extraordinary actions to avoid reaching the debt limit and to meet the federal government's other obligations. Some of the actions Treasury took during these periods are briefly discussed below.[13]

Actions in 1985

In September 1985, the Treasury Department informed Congress that it had reached the statutory debt limit. As a result, Treasury had to take extraordinary measures to meet the government's cash requirements. Treasury used various internal transactions involving the Federal Financing Bank (FFB) and delayed public auctions of government debt. It also was unable to issue, or had to delay issuing, new short-term government securities to the Civil Service Retirement and Disability Trust Fund, the Social Security Trust Funds, and several smaller trust funds. In particular, new Treasury obligations could not be issued to the trust funds because doing so would have exceeded the debt limit. Treasury took the additional step of "disinvesting" the Civil Service Retirement and Disability Trust Fund, the Social Security Trust Funds, and several smaller trust funds by redeeming some trust fund securities earlier than usual. Premature redemption of these securities created room under the debt ceiling for Treasury to borrow sufficient cash from the public to pay other obligations, including November 1985 Social Security benefits.[14] The debt limit was subsequently temporarily increased on November 14, 1985 (P.L. 99-155) and permanently increased on December 12, 1985 (P.L. 99-177) from $1,824 billion to $2,079 billion.

As a result of the 1985 debt limit crisis, Congress subsequently authorized Treasury to alter its normal investment and redemption procedures for certain trust funds during a debt limit crisis. Such authority was not provided with respect to the Social Security Trust Funds. In addition, both P.L. 99-155 and P.L. 99-177 included provisions to require Treasury to restore any interest income lost to the trust funds as a result of delayed investments and early redemptions.

---

[13] For a more detailed analysis of past Treasury actions surrounding the debt limit impasses of 1985, 1995-1996, and 2011, see the **Appendix**.

[14] Treasury also redeemed some of the Social Security Trust Funds' holdings of long-term securities to reimburse the General Fund for cash payments of benefits in September through November 1985. During this period, Treasury was unable to follow its normal procedure of issuing short-term securities to the trust funds and then redeeming short-term securities to reimburse the General Fund when it paid Social Security benefits.

Actions in 1995-1996

During the debt limit crisis of 1995-1996, Treasury, once again, used nontraditional methods of financing, including some of the methods used during the 1985 crisis as well as not reinvesting some of the maturing Treasury securities held by the Exchange Stabilization Fund.[15] In early 1996, Treasury announced that it had insufficient cash to pay Social Security benefits for March 1996, because it was unable to issue new public debt.[16] To allow benefits to be paid in March 1996, Congress authorized Treasury to issue securities to the public in the amount needed to make the March 1996 benefit payments and specified that, on a temporary basis, those securities would not count against the debt limit (P.L. 104-103 and P.L. 104-115). In 1996, Congress passed P.L. 104-121 to increase the debt limit and, among other provisions, to codify Congress's understanding that the Secretary of the Treasury and other federal officials are not authorized to use Social Security and Medicare funds for debt management purposes, except when necessary to provide for the payment of benefits or administrative expenses of the programs.

Actions in 2002-2003

During periods in 2002 and 2003 (from April 4 through April 16, 2002; from May 16 through June 28, 2002; and from February 20 through May 27, 2003), Treasury again took actions to avoid reaching the debt limit. These actions included utilizing certain trust fund assets and suspending the sale of securities to certain trust funds. The debt limit was permanently increased on June 28, 2002 (P.L. 107-199), from $5,950 billion to $6,400 billion and on May 27, 2003 (P.L. 108-24), from $6,400 billion to $7,384 billion.

Actions in 2009

Treasury used another tool in 2009 to cope with the debt limit without declaring a debt issuance suspension period. Specifically, Treasury used a program that was originally established as an alternative method for the Federal Reserve (Fed) to increase its assistance to the financial sector during the financial downturn, the Supplementary Financing Program (SFP). The SFP was announced on September 17, 2008. Under the SFP, Treasury temporarily auctioned more new securities than were needed to finance government operations and deposited the proceeds at the Fed. Beginning in January 2009, Treasury generally held $200 billion at the Fed under this program. When debt subject to limit approached the statutory debt limit around October 2009, however, Treasury withdrew all but $5 billion from the Fed to create room under the debt ceiling. Once the debt limit was raised on February 12, 2010, from $12,394 billion to $14,294 billion (P.L. 111-139), Treasury began increasing the balances held at the Fed back to $200 billion by

---

[15] Treasury's Exchange Stabilization Fund buys and sells foreign currency to promote exchange rate stability and counter disorderly conditions in the foreign exchange market.

[16] As described in the **Appendix**, under normal procedures Treasury pays Social Security benefits from the General Fund and offsets this by redeeming an equivalent amount of the trust funds' holdings of government debt. In order to pay Social Security benefits, and depending on the government's cash position at the time, Treasury may need to issue new public debt to raise the cash needed to pay benefits. Treasury may be unable to issue new public debt, however, because of the debt limit. Social Security benefit payments may be delayed or jeopardized if the Treasury does not have enough cash on hand to pay benefits.

issuing new debt to the public. As the debt limit was approached again, the SFP was reduced from $200 billion on February 2, 2011, to $5 billion on March 3, 2011, and to $0 on August 3, 2011.[17]

Treasury Actions Surrounding the Debt Limit Since 2011

Actions in 2011

Beginning in January 2011, Treasury again took actions to avoid reaching the debt limit and began notifying Congress of its intentions. On January 6, 2011, Treasury Secretary Geithner sent a letter to Congress stating that Treasury had the ability to delay the date by which the debt limit would be reached by utilizing similar methods used during past crises, including declaring a debt issuance suspension period, if necessary.[18] On May 2, 2011, Secretary Geithner issued another letter to Congress reiterating that the debt limit would be reached no later than May 16, 2011, but that the use of extraordinary measures would extend Treasury's ability to meet commitments through August 2, 2011.[19]

On Friday, May 6, the issuance of State and Local Government Series (SLGS) Treasury securities was suspended until further notice.[20] On May 16, 2011, Secretary Geithner notified Congress of his determination of a debt issuance suspension period and informed them of his intent to utilize extraordinary measures to create additional room under the debt ceiling to allow Treasury to continue funding the operations of the government.[21] Between May 16, 2011, and August 2, 2011, Treasury prematurely redeemed securities of the Civil Service Retirement and Disability Trust Fund and did not invest receipts of the Civil Service Retirement and Disability Trust Fund and the Postal Service Retiree Health Benefit Fund. Treasury also suspended investments in the Exchange Stabilization Fund and the Government Securities Investment Fund (G-Fund) of the Federal Thrift Savings Plan. Because these funds are required by law to be made whole once the debt limit is increased, these specific actions did not affect federal retirees or employees once the debt limit was increased.[22]

The debt limit was permanently increased on August 2, 2011, as part of the Budget Control Act of 2011 (BCA; P.L. 112-25), from $14,294 billion to $14,694 billion. The BCA provided for two

---

[17] The SFP has not been used since August 2011. Balances in the SFP account prior to that date can be found in Federal Reserve Bank, "Factors Affecting Reserve Balances," Table H.4.1, available at http://www.federalreserve.gov/releases/h41/.

[18] Letter from Timothy F. Geithner, Secretary of the Treasury, to the Hon. Harry Reid, Senate Majority Leader, January 6, 2011, available at http://www.treasury.gov/connect/blog/Pages/letter.aspx (hereinafter Treasury January 6th letter).

[19] Letter from Timothy F. Geithner, Secretary of the Treasury, to the Hon. John A. Boehner, Speaker of the House, May 2, 2011, available at http://www.treasury.gov/connect/blog/Documents/FINAL%20Debt%20Limit%20Letter%2005-02-2011%20Boehner.pdf (hereinafter Treasury May 2nd letter).

[20] For more information, see CRS Report R41811, *State and Local Government Series (SLGS) Treasury Debt: A Description*, by Steven Maguire.

[21] Letter from Timothy F. Geithner, Secretary of the Treasury, to the Hon. Harry Reid, Senate Majority Leader, May 16, 2011, available at http://www.treasury.gov/connect/blog/Documents/20110516Letter%20to%20Congress.pdf (hereinafter Treasury May 16th letter).

[22] Letter from Richard L. Gregg, Fiscal Assistant Secretary, Department of the Treasury, to the Hon. John A. Boehner, Speaker of the House, August 24, 2011, available at http://www.treasury.gov/initiatives/Documents/G%20Fund%20Letters.pdf and Letter to the Hon. Harry Reid, Senate majority leader, January 27, 2012, available at http://www.treasury.gov/initiatives/Documents/Debt%20Limit%20CSRDF%20Report%20to%20Reid.pdf.

---

additional debt limit increases. After the initial increase on August 2, 2011, the debt limit was permanently increased again on September 21, 2011, from $14,694 billion to $15,194 billion and again on January 27, 2012, from $15,194 billion to $16,394 billion.[23]

Actions in 2013

On December 26, 2012, Secretary Geithner sent a letter to Congress stating that the debt limit, the last increase provided for under the BCA, would be reached on December 31, 2012. Treasury estimated that the use of extraordinary measures would provide additional headroom under the debt limit until early 2013.[24] A debt issuance suspension period was declared on December 31, 2012, at which time Treasury prematurely redeemed securities of the Civil Service Retirement and Disability Trust Fund and did not invest receipts of the Civil Service Retirement and Disability Trust Fund and the Postal Service Retiree Health Benefit Fund.[25] On January 15, 2013, Secretary Geithner notified Congress that Treasury would suspend investments in the Government Securities Investment Fund (G-Fund) of the Federal Thrift Savings Plan.[26] On February 4, 2013, the statutory debt limit was suspended through May 18, 2013, as part of the No Budget, No Pay Act of 2013 (P.L. 113-3).

On May 19, 2013, the debt limit was reinstated and raised to $16,699 billion, a level which accommodated borrowing incurred during the suspension period.[27] The issuance of SLGS Treasury securities was suspended until further notice on May 15, 2013. A debt issuance suspension period was declared on May 20, 2013, at which time Treasury prematurely redeemed securities of the Civil Service Retirement and Disability Trust Fund and did not invest receipts of the Civil Service Retirement and Disability Trust Fund and the Postal Service Retiree Health Benefit Fund.[28] On May 31, 2013, Secretary Lew notified Congress that Treasury would suspend investments in the Government Securities Investment Fund (G-Fund) of the Federal Thrift

---

[23] For more information on the provisions providing for the debt limit to be increased under the BCA, see CRS Report R41965, *The Budget Control Act of 2011*, by Bill Heniff Jr., Elizabeth Rybicki, and Shannon M. Mahan. Prior to the third debt limit increase, investments in the Government Securities Investment Fund (G-Fund) of the Federal Thrift Savings Plan were suspended from January 17 to January 27, 2012. The G-Fund was made whole on January 27, 2012. Letter from Timothy F. Geithner, Secretary of the Treasury, to the Hon. Harry Reid, Senate Majority Leader, January 17, 2012, available at http://www.treasury.gov/initiatives/Documents/011712TFGLettertoReid.pdf.

[24] Letter from Timothy F. Geithner, Secretary of the Treasury, to the Hon. Harry Reid, Senate Majority Leader, December 26, 2012, available at http://www.treasury.gov/connect/blog/Documents/Sec%20Geithner%20LETTER%2012-26-2012%20Debt%20Limit.pdf.

[25] Letter from Timothy F. Geithner, Secretary of the Treasury, to the Hon. Harry Reid, Senate Majority Leader, December 31, 2012, available at http://www.treasury.gov/initiatives/Documents/Sec%20Geithner%20Letter%20to%20Congress%2012-31-2012.pdf.

[26] Letter from Timothy F. Geithner, Secretary of the Treasury, to the Hon. John A. Boehner, Speaker of the House, January 15, 2013, available at http://www.treasury.gov/initiatives/Documents/1-15-2013%20G%20Fund%20Debt%20Limit%20Letter.pdf.

[27] P.L. 113-3 provided for the debt limit to be increased on May 19, 2103 "to the extent that—(1) the face amount of obligations issued under chapter 31 of such title and the face amount of obligations whose principal and interest are guaranteed by the United States Government (except guaranteed obligations held by the Secretary of the Treasury) outstanding on May 19, 2013, exceeds (2) the face amount of such obligations outstanding on the date of the enactment of this Act. An obligation shall not be taken into account under paragraph (1) unless the issuance of such obligation was necessary to fund a commitment incurred by the Federal Government that required payment before May 19, 2013."

[28] Letter from Jacob J. Lew, Secretary of the Treasury, to the Hon. John A. Boehner, Speaker of the House, May 20, 2013, available at http://www.treasury.gov/initiatives/Documents/Debt%20Limit%20Letter%202%20Boehner%20May%2020%202013.pdf.

Savings Plan.[29] On October 1, 2013, Treasury estimated that the extraordinary measures would be exhausted "no later than October 17, 2013."[30] On October 17, 2013, the debt limit was suspended through February 7, 2014, as part of the Continuing Appropriations Act, 2014 (P.L. 113-46).

Observations from Past Actions

As discussed above, short delays in increasing the debt limit have caused the Treasury Secretary to take extraordinary actions to avoid disrupting the payments of federal obligations. Though the federal government incurred additional costs during these periods, such as disruption of government borrowing and trust fund investment programs, the payment of benefits and other outlays occurred largely on schedule and trust funds were made whole once these crises ended.[31] As long as the budget continues to be in deficit and policy makers wish to avoid a default on federal obligations, methods such as those described above cannot circumvent the need to eventually raise the debt limit.

Potential Implications of Reaching and Not Raising the Debt Limit

If the federal government were to reach the debt limit and Treasury were to exhaust its alternative strategies for remaining under the debt limit, then the federal government would need to rely solely on incoming revenues to finance obligations. If this occurred during a period when the federal government was running a deficit, the dollar amount of newly incurred federal obligations would continually exceed the dollar amount of newly incoming revenues.

It is not possible for CRS to specifically predict what Congress, the President, the Office of Management and Budget (OMB), Treasury, federal agencies, and financial markets would do in certain situations. Nevertheless, it is possible to scope out some aspects of what *could* happen under a specific scenario, in which the federal government is no longer able to issue debt, has exhausted alternative sources of cash, and therefore is dependent upon incoming receipts or other sources of funds to provide any cash that is necessary to pay federal obligations. That said, CRS cannot state the full range of events that may occur if the described scenario were to actually take place.

In this scenario, the federal government implicitly would be required to use some sort of decision-making rule about whether to pay obligations in the order they are received, or, alternatively, to prioritize which obligations to pay, while other obligations would go into an unpaid queue. In other words, the federal government's inability to borrow or use other means of financing implies that payment of some or all bills or obligations would be delayed.

---

[29] Letter from Jacob J. Lew, Secretary of the Treasury, to the Hon. John A. Boehner, Speaker of the House, May 31, 2013, available at http://www.treasury.gov/initiatives/Documents/ Debt%20Limit%20G%20Fund%2020130531%20Boehner.pdf.

[30] Letter from Jacob J. Lew, Secretary of the Treasury, to the Hon. John A. Boehner, Speaker of the House, October 1, 2013, available at http://www.treasury.gov/initiatives/Documents/Treasury%20Letter%20to%20Congress_100113.pdf.

[31] For a discussion of how Treasury's cash management practices and borrowing costs were affected during previous debt limit event periods, see GAO, *Delays Create Debt Management Challenges and Increase Uncertainty in the Treasury Market*, GAO-11-203, February 2011, pp. 10-18.

Possible Options for Treasury: Could Prioritization Be Used?

Some have argued that prioritization of payments can be used by Treasury to avoid a default on selected federal obligations by paying interest on outstanding debt before other obligations.[32] Treasury officials have maintained that the department lacks formal legal authority to establish priorities to pay obligations, asserting, in effect, that each law obligating funds and authorizing expenditures stands on an equal footing.[33] In other words, Treasury would have to make payments on obligations as they come due. With regard to this view, Treasury noted in 2011 that an attempt to prioritize payments was "unworkable" because adopting a policy that would require certain types of payments taking precedence over other U.S. legal obligations would merely be "a failure by the U.S. to stand behind its commitments."[34] In an August 2012 letter, the Treasury Inspector General also addressed this topic by stating, "Treasury officials determined that there is no fair or sensible way to pick and choose among the many bills that come due every day. Furthermore, because Congress has never provided guidance to the contrary, Treasury's systems are designed to make each payment in the order it comes due."[35] At a hearing before the Senate Finance Committee in October 2013, Treasury Secretary Lew stated the following:

> We write roughly 80 million checks a month. The systems are automated to pay because for 224 years, the policy of Congress and every president has been we pay our bills. You cannot go into those systems and easily make them pay some things and not other things. They weren't designed that way because it was never the policy of this government to be in the position that we would have to be in if we couldn't pay all our bills.[36]

In contrast to this view, GAO wrote to then-Chairman Bob Packwood of the Senate Finance Committee in 1985 that it was aware of no requirement that Treasury must pay outstanding obligations in the order in which they are received.[37] GAO concluded that "Treasury is free to liquidate obligations in any order it finds will best serve the interests of the United States." In any case, if Treasury were to prioritize, it is not clear what the priorities might be among the different types of spending.[38]

---

[32] A more in-depth discussion of these proposals and their implications can be found in the section titled "Views on the Debt Limit, Prioritization, and Default."

[33] U.S. Congress, Senate Committee on Finance, *Increase of Permanent Public Debt Limit*, S.Rpt. 99-144, September 26, 1985. For more information, see out-of-print CRS Report 95-1109, *Authority to Tap Trust Funds and Establish Payment Priorities if the Debt Limit is Not Increased*, by Thomas J. Nicola and Morton Rosenberg (available from CRS upon request).

[34] "Treasury: Proposals to 'Prioritize' Payments on U.S. Debt Not Workable: Would Not Prevent Default," Neal Wolin, Deputy Secretary of the Treasury, January 21, 2011, at http://www.treasury.gov/connect/blog/Pages/Proposals-to-Prioritize-Payments-on-US-Debt-Not-Workable-Would-Not-Prevent-Default.aspx.

[35] Letter from Eric M. Thorson, Chair, Council of the Inspectors General on Financial Oversight, to Hon. Orrin G. Hatch, ranking Member, Committee on Finance, August 24, 2012, Enclosure 1, pp. 5-6, available at http://www.treasury.gov/about/organizational-structure/ig/Audit%20Reports%20and%20Testimonies/Debt%20Limit%20Response%20(Final%20with%20Signature).pdf.

[36] U.S. Congress, Hearing of the Senate Committee on Finance, *The Debt Limit*, 113th Congress, 1st Session, October 10, 2013. Transcript available on CQ.com at http://www.cq.com/doc/congressionaltranscripts-4359941.

[37] Letter from GAO to the Hon. Bob Packwood, chairman of Senate Finance Committee, GAO B-138524, October 9, 1985, at http://redbook.gao.gov/14/fl0065142.php.

[38] While CRS has not located a list of established priorities to pay bills during a lapse in increasing the debt limit, OMB previously prepared a list of excepted functions that the government should continue to conduct during a government shutdown caused by a lapse in enacting appropriations. These priorities are based on a distinction between functions deemed essential and thus excepted, such as providing health care or air traffic control, and those deemed non-(continued...)

While the positions of Treasury and GAO may appear at first glance to differ, closer analysis suggests that they merely offer two different interpretations of silence in statute with respect to a prioritization system for paying obligations. On one hand, GAO's 1985 opinion posits that silence in statute with regard to prioritization simply leaves the determination of payment prioritization to the discretion of the Treasury Department. Conversely, Treasury appears to assert that the lack of specific statutory direction operates as a legal barrier, effectively preventing it from establishing a prioritization system.

Another perspective on prioritization relates to the Impoundment Control Act of 1974 (ICA), as amended.[39] The term *impoundment* refers to actions by the President, OMB, an agency head, or any officer or employee to preclude obligation or expenditure of budget authority. One type of impoundment action, *deferral*, refers to a temporary withholding or delaying of the obligation or expenditure of budget authority provided for projects or activities, or any other type of executive action or inaction which effectively precludes the obligation or expenditure of budget authority. Through the establishment of several statutory processes and restrictions, the ICA generally prohibited the use of discretion to effect "policy" impoundments. A policy impoundment might be, for example, a decision not to spend funds appropriated by Congress because a given federal activity may not be favored by a sitting President or agency official. Funds may be deferred only for certain reasons specified in 2 U.S.C. 684(b) (e.g., contingencies).[40] The relationship between prioritization associated with a debt limit impasse, on one hand, and the ICA, on the other, is that prioritization could be characterized as undertaking some spending but, due to lack of cash, deferring other spending.

In the event of a debt limit impasse, however, if the prioritization appears to disfavor certain programs, issues similar to those that gave rise to the ICA might resurface. These issues could include the balance of power between Congress and the President over spending priorities and the potential for use of prioritization in ways that Congress might not intend.[41] For example, if

---

(...continued)

excepted. If it should become necessary to establish priorities to pay bills when the debt limit has not been increased, it is possible that the Secretary of the Treasury may look to this list of essential functions for some guidance. For OMB's guidance on what activities are essential during a shutdown, see Sylvia Burwell, "Memorandum for the Heads of Executive Departments and Agencies," Office of Management and Budget, Sep. 17, 2013, http://www.whitehouse.gov/sites/default/files/omb/memoranda/2013/m-13-22.pdf. See also the later discussion in the section titled "Distinction Between a Debt Limit Crisis and a Government Shutdown."

[39] Title X of the Congressional Budget and Impoundment Control Act of 1974 (P.L. 93-344; 88 Stat. 297, at 332, and subsequently amended; 2 U.S.C. Chapter 17B, §681 et seq.). The act grew out of extended conflict over spending priorities between Congress and the Richard M. Nixon Administration, including over "policy" impoundments, where the Administration sought to not spend funds associated with disfavored programs. The act generally has been interpreted as being intended to protect congressional budget decisions and priorities, as manifest in statutes, from deviations by the President, OMB, and agency officials. For discussion, see Allen Schick, *Congress and Money: Budgeting, Spending, and Taxing* (Washington, DC: Urban Institute, 1980), pp. 17-49, 401-412.

[40] The ICA does not prohibit impoundments, but rather controls them. Among other things, the ICA established a mechanism for the President, the Director of OMB, the head of an agency, or any officer or employee to propose deferrals, for which the President is required to transmit a special message to each chamber of Congress with certain information. In addition, a deferral may not be proposed for any period of time extending beyond the end of the fiscal year in which the special message is transmitted.

[41] For related discussion, see Laurence H. Tribe, "Guest Post on the Debt Ceiling by Laurence Tribe," July 16, 2011, at http://www.dorfonlaw.org/2011/07/guest-post-on-debt-ceiling-by-laurence.html; and Neil H. Buchanan and Michael C. Dorf, "How to Choose the Least Unconstitutional Option: Lessons for the President (and Others) From the Debt Ceiling Standoff," *Columbia Law Review*, vol. 112, no. 6, October 2012, pp. 1175-1243, at http://www.columbialawreview.org/wp-content/uploads/2012/10/Buchanan-Dorf.pdf.

spending for a program that uses one-year funds were deferred until the end of a fiscal year, when the underlying budget authority expires, the deferral might constitute a functional equivalent of a rescission (cancellation of budget authority), akin to a line-item veto.[42] It appears that OMB and the Department of Justice have grappled with some of these issues in the past without coming to firm resolution, as evidenced by a 1995 internal OMB memorandum that was publicly released with papers of former White House Associate Counsel and current Supreme Court Justice Elena Kagan.[43]

Possible Options for OMB: Could Apportionment Be Used?

It also is possible that OMB may use statutory authority to apportion or reapportion budget authority (i.e., the authority to incur obligations) that Congress has granted in appropriations, contract, and borrowing authority to delay expenditures and effectively establish priorities for liquidating obligations. OMB is required by statute to "apportion" these funds (e.g., quarterly) to prevent agencies from spending at a rate that would exhaust their appropriations before the end of the fiscal year.[44] If OMB were to use statutory apportionment authority to affect the rate of federal spending, its ability to do so would be constrained by the Impoundment Control Act of 1974, as amended.[45] As noted earlier, the Impoundment Control Act does not prohibit the President from withholding funds, but establishes procedures for the President to submit formal requests to Congress either to defer (i.e., delay) spending until later or to rescind (i.e., cancel) the budget authority that Congress previously had granted.[46] Although the use of OMB's apportionment

---

[42] See related discussion in ibid. As noted earlier, the ICA provides that deferrals may not be proposed for any period of time extending beyond the end of the fiscal year in which the special message is transmitted. However, a debt limit impasse may create a situation in which it is impossible for the President or an agency official to comply with all aspects of existing law at the same time. Neil H. Buchanan and Michael C. Dorf characterized a debt ceiling standoff as a "trilemma," in which officials in the executive branch are offered "three unconstitutional options: ignore the debt ceiling and unilaterally issue new bonds, thus usurping Congress's borrowing power; unilaterally raise taxes, thus usurping Congress's taxing power; or unilaterally cut spending, thus usurping Congress's spending power." Ibid., p. 1175.

[43] See Office of Management and Budget, "Background Material on Prior Debt Ceiling Crises," memorandum from Roz Rettman to Bob Damus, August 2, 1995, pp. 4-5, as paginated within the document, which is available as pp. 7-11 of a PDF file, at http://www.clintonlibrary.gov/_previous/KAGAN%20COUNSEL/Counsel%20-%20Box%20006%20-%20Folder%20011.pdf. The OMB memorandum's author and recipient were senior career officials at OMB at the time. Elena Kagan currently is serving as Associate Justice of the U.S. Supreme Court. In 1995-1996, she served as Associate White House Counsel under President Clinton. Access to certain records from Justice Kagan's time in the Office of White House Counsel is provided at the Clinton Library website.

[44] 31 U.S.C. §1512, a provision of the Antideficiency Act, for example, states that appropriations for a definite period must be apportioned by such things as months, activities, or a combination of them to avoid obligation at a rate that would indicate a necessity of a deficiency or supplemental appropriations for the period. While apportionment commonly is used to control the rate at which agencies are allowed to *obligate* funds such as by placing orders and signing contracts, the text of Section 1512 also provides that it may be used to avoid *expending* funds.

[45] See 2 U.S.C. §§681-692. During the period leading up to enactment of the Impoundment Control Act of 1974, the Nixon Administration used apportionment authority as a tool ultimately to limit outlays to conform to the President's budgetary priorities. Several lawsuits were brought to challenge the President's authority not to expend funds that Congress had appropriated, and some lower courts held that the President lacked this authority. The Supreme Court did not address the merits of this issue.

[46] Generally, funds that have been proposed for deferral or rescission may be withheld from obligation for 45 days of continuous legislative session (excluding periods of more than three days when Congress is not in session), after which period the funds must be released unless Congress enacts a joint resolution to acquiesce in whole or in part to these requests. Congress sometimes responds to presidential deferral or rescission requests by acting on bills to defer or rescind different budget authorities from the ones that the President has proposed. Because deferrals or rescissions proposed by the President do not take effect unless Congress acquiesces to them, Congress as a matter of law has the (continued...)

---

authority in the event of a debt limit crisis might delay the need to pay some obligations, use of the authority would not prevent obligations from remaining unpaid.

Potential Impacts on Government Operations

If the debt limit is reached and not increased, federal spending would be affected. Under normal circumstances, Treasury has sufficient financial resources to liquidate all obligations arising from discretionary and mandatory (direct) spending, the latter of which includes interest payments on the debt.[47] If a lapse in raising the debt limit should prevent Treasury from being able to liquidate all obligations on time, it is not clear whether the distinction between different types of spending would be significant or whether the need to establish priorities would disproportionately impact one type of spending or another. It is also not clear whether the distinctions among different types of obligations, such as contract, grant, benefit, and interest payments, would prove to be significant.

Potential Impacts on Programs Generally

A government that delays paying its obligations in effect borrows from vendors, contractors, beneficiaries, other governments,[48] or employees who are not paid on time. Moreover, a backlog of unpaid bills would continue to grow until the government collects more revenues or other sources of cash than its outlays. In some cases, delaying federal payments incurs interest penalties under some statutes such as the Prompt Payment Act, which directs the government to pay interest penalties to contractors if it does not pay them by the required payment date,[49] and the Internal Revenue Code, which requires the government to pay interest penalties if tax refunds are delayed beyond a certain date.[50] The specific impacts of delayed payment would depend upon the nature of the federal program or activity for which funds are to be paid.

(...continued)

final say on these matters. In practice, however, funds that are subject to these presidential requests often are withheld for long periods because of congressional recesses, which as noted above are not counted for purposes of the ICA. For more information, see CRS Report RL33869, *Rescission Actions Since 1974: Review and Assessment of the Record*, by Virginia A. McMurtry, p. 2.

[47] Discretionary spending is provided in, and controlled by, annual appropriations acts, which fund many of the routine activities commonly associated with such federal government functions as running executive branch agencies, congressional offices and agencies, and international operations of the government. Mandatory spending includes federal government spending on entitlement programs as well as other budget outlays controlled by laws other than appropriations acts. Mandatory spending also includes appropriated entitlements, such as Medicaid and certain veterans' programs, which are funded in annual appropriations acts. For more information, see CRS Report RS20129, *Entitlements and Appropriated Entitlements in the Federal Budget Process*, by Bill Heniff Jr.

[48] For example, because federal, state, and local government finances are linked by various intergovernmental transfers, late payment or nonpayment of federal obligations to states could affect the budgets and finances of local governments, such as school districts, counties, and municipalities.

[49] 31 U.S.C. §3902. The Prompt Payment Act generally requires federal agencies to pay interest on any payments they fail to make by the date(s) specified in a contract or within 30 days of a receipt of a proper invoice. For more information, see the section titled "The Prompt Payment Act" in CRS Report R41230, *Legal Protections for Subcontractors on Federal Prime Contracts*, by Kate M. Manuel.

[50] 26 U.S.C. §6611.

Potential Impacts on Programs with Trust Funds

If Treasury delays investing a federal trust fund's revenues in government securities, or redeems prematurely a federal trust fund's holdings of government securities, the result would be a loss of interest to the affected trust fund. This could potentially worsen the financial situation of the affected trust fund(s) and accelerate insolvency dates.[51] As noted earlier, Congress passed P.L. 104-121 to prevent federal officials from using the Social Security and Medicare Trust Funds for debt management purposes, except when necessary to provide for the payment of benefits and administrative expenses of the programs. Under P.L. 99-509, Treasury is permitted to delay investment in the TSP's G-Fund and the Civil Service Retirement and Disability Trust Fund, and also to redeem prematurely assets of the Civil Service Retirement and Disability Trust Fund. However, the law also requires Treasury to make these funds whole after a debt limit impasse is resolved. The government maintains a number of other trust funds whose finances could potentially be harmed by delayed investment or early redemption in the absence of similar actions to make the trust funds whole after a debt limit impasse has ended.

Distinction Between a Debt Limit Crisis and a Government Shutdown

In 1995, the Congressional Budget Office (hereinafter CBO) contrasted this sort of scenario, under which the debt limit is reached and not raised, with a substantially different situation, in which the government must shut down due to lack of appropriations.

> Failing to raise the debt ceiling would not bring the government to a screeching halt the way that not passing appropriations bills would. Employees would not be sent home, and checks would continue to be issued. If the Treasury was low on cash, however, there could be delays in honoring checks and disruptions in the normal flow of government services.[52]

Alternatively stated, in a situation when the debt limit is reached and Treasury exhausts its financing alternatives, aside from ongoing cash flow, an agency may continue to obligate funds. However, Treasury may not be able to liquidate all obligations that result in federal outlays due to a shortage of cash. In contrast to this, if Congress and the President do not enact interim or full-year appropriations for an agency, the agency does not have budget authority available for obligation. If this occurs, the agency must shut down non-excepted activities, with immediate effects on government services.[53]

Potential Economic and Financial Effects

In addition to the potential impact on federal programs and activities if the debt limit is not increased, there may also be economic and financial consequences. A 1979 GAO report described the consequences of failing to increase the debt ceiling. GAO said the government had never defaulted on any of its securities, because cash has been available to pay interest and redeem

---

[51] For information about the balances of all federal trust funds, see CRS Report R41328, *Federal Trust Funds and the Budget*, by Thomas L. Hungerford.

[52] CBO, *The Economic and Budget Outlook: An Update*, August 1995, p. 49.

[53] In the event of a funding hiatus, the Antideficiency Act nevertheless allows an exception for agencies to incur obligations for emergencies involving the safety of human life or the protection of property. For a discussion, see CRS Report RL34680, *Shutdown of the Federal Government: Causes, Processes, and Effects*, coordinated by Clinton T. Brass.

---

them upon maturity or demand.[54] Further, GAO said a default on the securities could have adverse effects on the economy, the public welfare, and the government's ability to market future securities.

> It is difficult to perceive all the adverse effects that a government default for even a short time would have on the economy and the public welfare. It is generally recognized that a default would preclude the government from honoring all of its obligations to pay for such things as employees' salaries and wages; social security benefits, civil service retirement, and other benefits from trust funds; contractual services and supplies, and maturing securities.... At a minimum, however, the government could be subject to additional claims for interest on unredeemed matured debt and to claims for damages resulting from failure to make payments. But even beyond that, the full faith and credit of the U.S. government would be threatened. Domestic money markets, in which government securities play a major role, could be affected substantially.[55]

If the debt limit were reached and interest payments on debt were paid, it is not clear what the repercussions would be on the financial markets or the economy. If Treasury had to rely on incoming cash to pay its obligations, a significant portion of government spending would go unpaid. Removing a portion of government spending from the economy would leave behind significant economic effects and would have an effect on gross domestic product (GDP) by definition, all other things being equal.[56] Further, if the government fails to make timely payments to individuals, service providers, and other organizations, these persons and entities would also be affected. Even if the government continued paying interest, it is not clear whether creditors would retain or lose faith in the government's willingness to pay its obligations. If creditors lost this confidence, the federal government's interest costs would likely increase substantially and there would likely be broader disruptions to financial markets.

On April 25, 2011, the Treasury Borrowing Advisory Committee[57] sent a letter to Secretary Geithner expressing its views on the impact on financial markets if the debt ceiling is not raised.[58] The letter warned that any delay by Treasury in making an interest or principal payment could trigger "another catastrophic financial crisis." Further, the committee described several potential consequences stemming from a Treasury default on its obligations including a downgrade of the U.S. credit rating, an increase in federal and private borrowing costs, damage to the economic recovery, and broader disruptions to the financial system. Finally, the committee also warned that a prolonged delay in raising the debt limit could have negative consequences on the market before the time when default would actually occur.[59]

---

[54] While this passage indicates that a delay in increasing the debt limit has the potential to postpone the payment of Social Security benefits, among other benefits, Social Security benefits have been paid on time during past debt limit crises. Non-marketable securities can be redeemed on demand. GAO, *A New Approach to the Public Debt Legislation Should be Considered*, FGMSD-79-58, September 1979, pp. 17-18, http://archive.gao.gov/f0302/110373.pdf.

[55] Ibid.

[56] GDP = consumption + investment + government spending + (exports – imports). If government spending declines, then GDP will also decline by definition, all else equal.

[57] The Treasury Borrowing Advisory Committee is a group of senior representatives from investment funds and banks that presents its observations on the overall strength of the U.S. economy and provides recommendations on a variety of technical debt management issues to the Treasury Department.

[58] More information on the Treasury Borrowing Advisory Committee can be found at http://www.treasury.gov/resource-center/data-chart-center/quarterly-refunding/Pages/default.aspx.

[59] Letter from Matthew E. Zames, Chairman of Treasury Borrowing Advisory Committee, to Timothy F. Geithner, April 25, 2011, available at http://www.sifma.org/issues/item.aspx?id=25013.

Effects of 2011 and 2013 "Brinkmanship"[60]

Extended debate over whether or not to raise the debt limit can also have financial and economic consequences even if the debt limit does eventually get raised. While not causing financial instability, what has been referred to as "brinkmanship" can lead to worse economic or financial outcomes than raising the debt limit well ahead of time. While the debt limit impasse has no direct effect on the economy because it does not interfere with government financing, it could still have had indirect effects on GDP and financial conditions if it altered the behavior of households and businesses.

The effects of "brinkmanship" can be answered by observing what happened to the economy and financial markets during the 2011 and 2013 debt limit impasse. Neither episode caused financial disruption or recession (although, in the case of 2013, GDP data are not yet released).[61] Nevertheless, both episodes had discernible effects. Economic growth in the third quarter of 2011 was noticeably slower (1.4%) than the preceding or following quarter, although it is difficult to isolate how much of that slowdown could be attributed to the debt limit impasse.[62] The Treasury Department released a report detailing how the August 2011 debt limit impasse coincided with a marked decline in consumer confidence, small business optimism, and the S&P 500 stock index, and an increase in the equity market volatility index ("VIX"). In each case, these indicators did not return to their previous levels until several months after the debt limit was raised.[63] The Treasury report does not attempt to isolate the effects of the debt limit impasse from other events that would also affect financial markets concurrently. Notably, the debt limit impasse also resulted in the first downgrade of federal debt by a major credit rating agency, when Standard & Poor's downgraded the debt from AAA on August 5, 2011. In its statement on the downgrade, S&P said that

> More broadly, the downgrade reflects our view that the effectiveness, stability, and predictability of American policymaking and political institutions have weakened at a time of ongoing fiscal and economic challenges to a degree more than we envisioned...[64]

Thus, as their statement would suggest, another channel through which the debt limit might affect private spending is via heightened policy uncertainty.

By contrast, however, those same indicators showed a much smaller deterioration in October 2013. Consumer confidence also fell in October 2013, although this may have been partly caused by the concurrent government shutdown. It remained at higher levels than in August 2011 or during the financial crisis, however. The S&P 500 stock index fell by less than 3% during the shutdown, but had recovered its previous value by the time the government was reopened. This suggests that either investors felt more confident that the debt limit would ultimately be raised

---

[60] This section was written by Marc Labonte, Specialist in Macroeconomic Policy.

[61] The absence of large declines in financial markets could be interpreted as a market belief that a default would not have serious effects or that "brinkmanship" is unlikely to result in a default because the debt limit will ultimately be raised.

[62] The fact that growth accelerated in the following quarter suggests that the debt limit impasse did not have prolonged effects on the economy.

[63] U.S. Treasury, *The Potential Macroeconomic Effect of Debt Ceiling Brinkmanship*, Oct. 2013.

[64] Standard & Poors, "United States of America Long-Term Rating Lowered to AA+ Due to Political Risks, Rising Debt Burden; Outlook Negative," August 5, 2011, available at http://www.standardandpoors.com/ratings/articles/en/us/?assetID=1245316529563.

(perhaps because it had been raised in similar circumstances in 2011) or other factors, such as the downgrade, are responsible for the greater deterioration in credit markets in August 2011.[65]

The two financial instruments that experienced the most pronounced price movements in the 2011 and 2013 debt limit impasses were short-term Treasury securities and credit default swaps (CDS) on U.S. Treasuries. First, Treasury yields exhibited a highly unusual pattern. For example, from October 1 to October 16, 2013, yields on Treasury bills maturing in four weeks exceeded those maturing in three months. The consensus explanation for this phenomenon was fear that a failure to raise the debt limit in a timely fashion could cause short-term interruptions in repaying maturing debt, and the unusual pattern disappeared as soon as the debt limit was raised. (The rest of the yield curve has not exhibited any unusual movements recently.) Nevertheless, the yield on 4-week bills (0.32% on October 15) implied that this risk was still perceived to be relatively low. Since noticeably higher rates were not manifested throughout the rest of the Treasury yield curve, the broader economic consequences of this anomaly were likely limited. Their main effect was to directly raise the borrowing costs of the Treasury on securities sold during the period of elevated yields. In the 2011 debt limit impasse, GAO estimated that the debt limit impasse increased Treasury borrowing costs by $1.3 billion in 2011.[66]

Second, CDS prices for which Treasury securities are the reference entity rose significantly. Credit default swaps for which federal debt is the reference entity would trigger a payment from the seller of the CDS to the buyer if the security experiences a "credit event" related to timely and full payment.[67] In 2011, CDS prices for five-year Treasury securities (i.e., the cost to insure against default) rose above 60 basis points, for example; this level was unusually high compared with historical standards, but lower than at the depth of the 2008 financial crisis.[68] At its peak on October 10, 2013, CDS prices for five-year Treasury securities more than doubled compared to the previous month, rising to 40 basis points; this price was below the peak price in 2011.[69]

Economic indicators covering the 2013 debt limit impasse will not be available for some time, and it will be difficult to disentangle the effects of the debt limit impasse from the effects of the government shutdown, which happened simultaneously.

---

[65] There was also a marked decline in Treasury yields in August 2011; since this was not matched by a decline in private yields, it caused the spread between Treasury yields and private yields to widen. Based on the timing, this movement appears to have been in response to the downgrade rather than the debt limit impasse, and so is attributable to the debt limit impasse only in the sense that it triggered the downgrade.

[66] This estimate includes only costs incurred in FY2011. It does not include any additional interest costs incurred in future years on outstanding securities related to this borrowing. See Government Accountability Office, *Analysis of 2011-2012 Actions Taken and Effect of Delayed Increase on Borrowing Costs*, report number GAO-12-701, July 23, 2012.

[67] The circumstances under which CDS on Treasury securities would be triggered are described in International Swaps and Derivatives Association, *CDS on US Sovereign Debt- FAQ*, updated Oct. 9, 2013.

[68] Abigail Moses, "U.S. Credit-Default Swaps Trading Surges 80% as Debt Deadline Approaches," *Bloomberg*, July 28, 2011. For more information on Treasury CDS in 2011 and the pricing of CDS, see CRS Report R41932, *Treasury Securities and the U.S. Sovereign Credit Default Swap Market*, by D. Andrew Austin and Rena S. Miller.

[69] Markit, *Biggest Credit Movers*, Oct. 10, 2013, http://www.markit.com/assets/en/docs/commentary/markit-movers/Biggest%20Credit%20Movers%20Import/BigMovers_101013.pdf.

Considerations for the Current Debt Limit Debate

There are various viewpoints about how to deal with debt limit issues. The debt subject to limit will generally continue to rise as long as the budget remains in deficit and/or trust funds remain in surplus. To avoid raising the debt limit and continue normal government operations, significant spending cuts and/or revenue increases would be required.

Views on the Debt Limit, Prioritization, and Default

Members of the Obama Administration have maintained that not raising the debt limit would cause serious consequences. Former Treasury Secretary Geithner repeatedly asserted that not increasing the debt limit and, therefore, not meeting the country's obligations as a result "would cause irreparable harm to the American economy and to the livelihoods of all Americans."[70] President Obama has also repeatedly stated that the debt limit must be raised and he will not negotiate on this issue. He stated, "The financial well-being of the American people is not leverage to be used. The full faith and credit of the United States of America is not a bargaining chip."[71]

Speaker of the House John A. Boehner has stated that the debt limit should not be increased without "spending cuts or reforms" greater than the amount of the increase.[72] Senate Majority Leader Harry Reid has stated that he will require a balanced approach to dealing with the budget deficit and the debt with spending cuts paired with "revenue measures asking millionaires to pay their fair share." In the absence of an agreement to this effect, he remains committed to the spending cuts already in place.[73]

Economists have expressed concern regarding the current level of federal debt. However, they generally maintain that there would be significant consequences if the debt limit is not raised. Federal Reserve Chairman Ben Bernanke has stated that Congress must work to put a plan in to place that would lower the nation's federal debt. He also stated that not raising the debt limit could ultimately lead the nation to default on its debt with catastrophic implications for the financial system and the economy.[74] Mark Zandi, chief economist for Moody's Analytics, expressed similar sentiments regarding the debt limit and the potential impact on the economy. He stated, "Global investors are already anxious regarding our ability to come to a political consensus to address the nation's fiscal challenges; a protracted debate over the debt ceiling would be very counterproductive."[75] Donald Marron, the former director of the Urban-Brookings

---

[70] Letter from Timothy F. Geithner, Secretary of the Treasury, to the Hon. John A. Boehner, Speaker of the U.S. House of Representatives, January 14, 2013, available at http://www.treasury.gov/connect/blog/Documents/1-14-13%20Debt%20Limit%20FINAL%20LETTER%20Boehner.pdf.

[71] "President Obama Holds the Final Press Conference of His First Term," January 14, 2013, available at http://www.whitehouse.gov/blog/2013/01/14/president-obama-holds-final-press-conference-his-first-term.

[72] Peter G. Peterson Foundation's 2012 Fiscal Summit, *Speaker Boehner's Address on the Economy, Debt Limit, and American Jobs*, May 15, 2012, available at http://www.speaker.gov/speech/full-text-speaker-boehners-address-economy-debt-limit-and-american-jobs.

[73] Cooper, Helene, "Obama and House Republicans Offer Taste of Renewed Fight Over the Debt Ceiling," *New York Times*, May 16, 2012.

[74] Davidson, Paul, "Economy still in a deep hole, Bernanke says," *USA Today*, February 4, 2011.

[75] U.S. Congress, Senate Committee on the Budget, *Challenges for the U.S. Economic Recovery*, Testimony of Mark Zandi, February 3, 2011, available at http://budget.senate.gov/democratic/testimony/2011/
(continued...)

Tax Policy Center and a former Acting Director of the Congressional Budget Office, expressed similar views in January 2011. He stated, "Geithner is correct that the debt limit must increase. With monthly deficits running more than $100 billion, it's simply unthinkable that Congress could cut spending or increase revenue enough to avoid borrowing more.... Still, I am troubled by any suggestion that the United States might willingly default on its public debt. Doing so would have absolutely no upside."[76]

Questions have been raised regarding what constitutes a legal "default" by the government. Some proponents of a prioritization system suggest that the term "default" applies only if the government fails to pay interest on debt obligations held by third parties. Opponents of prioritization appear to argue that the term "default" applies not only to a failure to pay third-party debt holders, but also to the failure by the government to meet any obligation authorized by law, which would include a failure to fund an appropriated program, pay federal salaries or benefits, or pay an amount owed on a federal contract. No general statutory definition of the term "default" exists; however, *Black's Law Dictionary* 428 (7th Ed. 1999) defines the term "default" as "the failure to make a payment when due," which, if accepted as the governing definition, would not appear to distinguish between various types of government obligations.

Aside from technical definitions, financial markets' perceptions of what constitutes a default, or a real threat of default, may be more relevant when assessing the potential impacts of not raising the debt limit. For example, if the federal government were to prioritize payments on debt obligations above other obligations, it is not clear whether financial markets would find this distinction to be significant when deciding whether and how to invest in federal government Treasury securities, since Treasury would be postponing payments on other legal obligations. Because perceptions such as these are difficult if not impossible to predict, it is not clear what the effects of prioritization would be, in the event of an impasse.[77] In the event of reaching the debt limit and the enactment of prioritization legislation, certain payments would receive priority. However, issues also might arise related to how a President, OMB, or an agency prioritizes among any obligations and expenditures that are not explicitly subject to prioritization, by statute. As noted earlier in this report, circumstances like these could prompt issues similar to those that gave rise to the Impoundment Control Act of 1974.

Legislative Action[78]

On April 30, 2013, the House Ways and Means Committee reported the Full Faith and Credit Act (H.R. 807, 113th Congress). This legislation, as reported by the committee, would require Treasury to prioritize payments on obligations of debt held by the public and to the Social Security Trust Funds in the event that the debt limit is reached and to provide weekly reports of these obligations. On May 9, 2013, the House approved this legislation by a vote of 221-207. A similar measure was included as part of proposed legislation to provide for appropriations for a

---

(...continued)

Zandi_Senate_Budget_2_3_2011.pdf.

[76] Marron, Donald, "Debt Ceiling: Geithner Won't Let Us Default," *CNNMoney.com*, January 19, 2011.

[77] The potential effects of reaching the debt limit on financial markets are further discussed in the section titled "Potential Economic and Financial Effects."

[78] This section contains descriptions of legislation that has been either reported by committee or considered in either the House or the Senate as it relates to the debt limit since the enactment of P.L. 113-3 (H.R. 325). Other bills related to prioritization of payments in the event the debt limit is reached have been introduced in the House and the Senate.

portion of FY2014 via a continuing resolution. The legislation, including this provision, was approved by the House on September 20, 2013 (H.J.Res. 59, 113th Congress) though ultimately not included in the final bill enacted into law.

Can an Increase in the Current Debt Limit Be Avoided?

Budget outlays and revenue collections over the fiscal year, along with the funds contained in the extraordinary measures, will affect the timing of the debate over raising the debt limit. The debt limit is currently suspended through February 7, 2014. In May 2013, CBO estimated that the federal government would have to issue an additional $728 billion in debt in FY2014 under current law.[79] If the current suspension period ends and the extraordinary measures are exhausted, Treasury will no longer be able to issue federal debt absent further legislative action. At that time, federal spending would have to be decreased or federal revenues would have to be increased by a corresponding amount to cover what cannot be borrowed.

If the debt limit is reached and the extraordinary measures are exhausted, incoming revenues would be the only way to finance obligations. To put this into context, the federal government is expected to spend roughly $100 billion per month on discretionary programs, $180 billion per month on mandatory programs, and $20 billion in interest, on average, in FY2014. Monthly revenue collections are expected to be roughly $250 billion, yielding a monthly deficit of roughly $50 billion. (Spending, revenue collection, and interest payments can vary significantly from month to month.) This means that discretionary spending would have to be cut by half or mandatory would have to be cut by 30% each month, or some combination of the two would have to occur to counteract the shortfall of what cannot be borrowed.[80] Alternatively, revenues could be increased by roughly 20% per month to cover the spending provided for in current law.[81]

This provides an approximation of what would be required to cover the average monthly borrowing need for FY2014. It does not address what would be required in future years to avoid further increases in the debt limit. Moreover, if Congress and the President enact legislation raising future levels of spending or lowering revenues without providing offsets, the borrowing needs of government would increase as the deficit grows larger.

How Much Should the Debt Limit Be Raised?

Under several current policy proposals, the debt subject to limit is projected to increase throughout the remainder of the decade. Under President Obama's FY2014 budget, the debt subject to limit is projected to reach $25,329 billion at the end of FY2023.[82] This represents an increase of roughly $800 billion, on average, in each fiscal year during the FY2014 to FY2023

---

[79] This amounts to an increase of $164 billion in new debt subject to limit in FY2013 relative to the current statutory debt limit ($16.699 trillion). CRS calculations based on CBO, *Updated Budget Projections: Fiscal Years 2013 to 2023*, May 2013, Table 5.

[80] The levels of spending discussed here assume that the discretionary spending caps and automatic spending reductions enacted under the BCA remain in place. These reductions in spending to cover borrowing needs would occur on top of the cuts already scheduled to take place under current law.

[81] CRS calculations based on CBO, *Updated Budget Projections: Fiscal Years 2013 to 2023*, May 2013, Table 1.

[82] Office of Management and Budget, *Budget of the U.S. Government, Fiscal Year 2014, The Budget*, Table S-13, available at http://www.whitehouse.gov/sites/default/files/omb/budget/fy2014/assets/tables.pdf.

---

period. Increases in debt subject to limit at this level occur even as the budget deficit is projected to decline, in nominal dollars, between FY2014 and FY2018. Between FY2019 and FY2023, the budget deficit is projected to remain roughly stable.[83] In other words, the debt subject to limit increases even if the budget deficit declines in nominal terms as issuing debt would still be required to finance the projected federal spending in excess of federal revenues.

According to the figures provided in the House Budget Committee report (H.Rept. 113-17) accompanying the House FY2014 Budget Resolution (H.Con.Res. 25, 113th Congress) agreed to on March 21, 2013, the debt subject to limit is projected to rise from $17,776 billion at the end of FY2014 to $20,320 billion at the end of FY2023. This means that, if the policies contained in the House-passed budget resolution were to be enacted, the debt limit would have to increase by $2,544 billion (or roughly $300 billion in each fiscal year) during the FY2014 to FY2023 period to accommodate these proposals.

According to the figures provided in the Senate Budget Committee print (S.Prt. 113-12) to accompany the Senate FY2014 Budget Resolution (S.Con.Res. 8, 113th Congress) agreed to on March 23, 2013, the gross debt is projected to rise from $18,008 billion at the end of FY2014 to $24,365 billion at the end of FY2023.[84] This means that, if the policies contained in the Senate-passed budget resolution were to be enacted, the debt limit would have to increase by $6,357 billion (or roughly $700 billion in each fiscal year) during the FY2014 to FY2023 period to accommodate these proposals.

Given the borrowing requirements under both the President's FY2014 budget and the House- and Senate-passed budget resolutions, the current estimates stipulate the increases in the debt limit that would be required. However, depending on the spending and revenue proposals that may be subsequently enacted, borrowing requirements could change going forward. These borrowing requirements will dictate the level of debt and future increases in the debt limit. How often Congress wishes to reconsider statutory debt limit legislation typically affects the level at which the debt limit is set.

Temporary increases in the debt limit have been used in the past to provide additional time for Congress to consider debt limit increases. However, past temporary debt limit increases were eventually followed by permanent increases. If a temporary increase were to expire and the debt limit were to revert to a prior lower level, Congress may want to enact legislation that would result in a budget surplus in excess of the intragovernmental surplus in order to lower the level of debt subject to limit. If this legislation is not enacted and fully realized prior to the expiration of the temporary limit, then the level of debt would exceed the lowered debt limit.

Implications of Future Federal Debt on the Debt Limit

It is extremely difficult for Congress to effectively influence short-term fiscal and budgetary policy through action on legislation adjusting the debt limit. For example, the debt could reach

---

[83] Ibid., Table S-1.

[84] The committee print did not provide figures on debt subject to limit, which is typically less than 1% lower than gross debt.

the statutory limit after spending and revenue decisions for the current fiscal year have already been made. The need to raise (or lower) the limit during a session of Congress is driven by previous decisions regarding revenues and spending. These decisions stem from legislation enacted earlier in the session or in prior years.

From the Congressional Budget Office (CBO):

> By itself, setting a limit on the debt is an ineffective means of controlling deficits because the decisions that necessitate borrowing are made through other legislative actions. By the time an increase in the debt ceiling comes up for approval, it is too late to avoid paying the government's pending bills without incurring serious negative consequences.[85]

Nevertheless, the consideration of debt limit legislation often is viewed as an opportunity to reexamine fiscal and budgetary policy. Consequently, House and Senate action on legislation adjusting the debt limit often is complicated, hindered by policy disagreements, and subject to delay.[86] Many in Congress have stated that the debt limit should not be raised without accompanying deficit reduction legislation.

Generally, the following scenarios dictate whether or not an increase in the debt limit would be necessary, all else constant:

- If the federal budget is in deficit and intragovernmental debt is rising, an increase in the debt limit would be necessary.

- If the federal budget is in deficit and intragovernmental debt falls by an amount that is smaller than the budget deficit, an increase in the debt limit would be necessary.

- If the federal budget is balanced or in surplus and intragovernmental debt rises by an amount that is larger than the budget surplus, an increase in the debt limit would be necessary.

- If the federal budget is balanced or in surplus and intragovernmental debt is falling, an increase in the debt limit would not be required.

In other words, increases in the statutory debt limit would be required if the budget remains in deficit, even if future deficit levels are lower than they are at present, or if there are increases in the level of intragovernmental debt. If intragovernmental debt is declining, presumably due to the need of certain trust funds to redeem their holdings of Treasury securities in order to pay benefits, Treasury would have to provide the trust funds with cash either from the General Fund resources or by issuing additional debt to the public to raise cash. If the federal budget is in deficit, Treasury would have to raise the necessary cash to redeem trust fund securities by issuing debt to the public. This would not require an increase in the debt limit, as the decline in intragovernmental debt would be offset by an equal increase in debt held by the public. A decline in intragovernmental debt as a result of a redemption in trust fund securities could be financed by using surplus cash if the federal budget is in surplus at that time.[87] In this situation, debt held by

---

[85] CBO, *Federal Debt and Interest Costs*, December 2010, p. 23, available at http://www.cbo.gov/ftpdocs/119xx/doc11999/12-14-FederalDebt.pdf.

[86] For more information, see CRS Report RS21519, *Legislative Procedures for Adjusting the Public Debt Limit: A Brief Overview*, by Bill Heniff Jr.

[87] Under the most recent projections, the federal budget is expected to remain in deficit through FY2023 under current (continued...)

---

the public, debt held by government accounts, and total federal debt would decrease. If the budget surplus were less than the reduction in intragovernmental debt, the increase in the debt held by the public would be offset by the decline in intragovernmental debt, resulting in a decrease in the total debt.

(...continued)
law. CBO, *The Budget and Economic Outlook: Fiscal Years 2013 to 2023*, February 2013, Table 1-1.

Appendix. Detailed History on Past Treasury Actions During Previous Debt Limit Crises

Selected Actions in 1985

In September 1985, the Treasury Department informed Congress that it had reached the statutory debt limit. As a result, Treasury had to take extraordinary measures to meet the government's cash requirements. Treasury used various internal transactions involving the Federal Financing Bank (FFB) and delayed public auctions of government debt. It also was unable to issue, or had to delay issuing, new short-term government securities to the Civil Service Retirement and Disability Trust Fund, the Social Security Trust Funds, and several smaller trust funds. Issuing new government securities to the trust funds would have caused the federal debt to exceed the debt limit. During this period, the bulk of Social Security payroll tax revenues were kept in a non-interest bearing account.

Treasury took the additional step of "disinvesting" the Civil Service Retirement and Disability Trust Fund, the Social Security Trust Funds, and several smaller trust funds by redeeming some trust fund securities earlier than usual. Premature redemption of these securities created room under the debt ceiling for Treasury to borrow sufficient cash from the public to pay other obligations, including November Social Security benefits.[88]

As a result of these various actions, Social Security benefit payments and other federal payments were not jeopardized. The debt limit was subsequently temporarily increased on November 14, 1985 (P.L. 99-155), and permanently increased on December 12, 1985 (P.L. 99-177), from $1,824 billion to $2,079 billion. Both P.L. 99-155 and P.L. 99-177 included provisions to require Treasury to restore any interest income lost to the trust funds as a result of delayed investments and early redemptions.

Concerning Treasury's management of the Social Security Trust Funds during the 1985 debt limit impasse, the General Accounting Office (GAO, now the Government Accountability Office) wrote: "We conclude that, although some of the Secretary's actions appear in retrospect to have been in violation of the requirements of the Social Security Act, we cannot say that the Secretary acted unreasonably given the extraordinary situation in which he was operating."[89] In particular, GAO found that not all the delayed investment and securities redemptions during the period from September through November 1985 were necessary to meet Social Security benefit payments, and the excess was used to finance general government operations.[90]

---

[88] Treasury redeemed some of the Social Security Trust Funds' holdings of long-term securities to reimburse the General Fund for cash payments of benefits in September through November 1985. During this period, the Treasury was unable to follow its normal procedure of issuing short-term securities to the trust funds and then redeeming short-term securities to reimburse the General Fund when it paid Social Security benefits.

[89] Letter from Charles A. Bowsher, Comptroller General of the United States, to the Hon. James R. Jones, chairman, Subcommittee on Social Security, House Committee on Ways and Means, December 5, 1985, GAO B-221077.2, http://archive.gao.gov/d12t3/128621.pdf.

[90] Ibid.

Following the 1985 debt limit crisis, Congress formally authorized the Secretary of the Treasury to declare a debt issuance suspension period and, during such periods, to depart from normal trust fund investment practices with respect to certain funds such as the Civil Service Retirement and Disability Fund and the TSP's G Fund (P.L. 99-509, the Omnibus Budget Reconciliation Act of 1986). Funds raised by procedures authorized during a debt issuance suspension period can only be used to the extent necessary to prevent the public debt from exceeding the debt limit. After the debt issuance suspension period has ended, P.L. 99-509 requires Treasury to make the trust funds whole by issuing the appropriate amount of securities and crediting any interest lost due to non-investment or early disinvestment of these funds.[91] Such authority to depart from normal trust fund investment practices was not provided with respect to the Social Security Trust Funds. A provision to allow such authority was dropped from P.L. 99-509 during conference.

Selected Actions in 1995-1996

Following the enactment of this additional authority, the first debt issuance suspension period was announced on November 15, 1995. Treasury, once again, used non-traditional methods of financing, including some of the methods used during the 1985 crisis as well as not reinvesting some of the maturing Treasury securities held by the Exchange Stabilization Fund.[92] In addition, Treasury utilized the new authority that was enacted under P.L. 99-509 to declare a debt issuance suspension period.

In early 1996, Treasury announced that it had insufficient cash to pay Social Security benefits for March 1996.[93] Congress responded on February 1, 1996, by passing P.L. 104-103, which provided Treasury with temporary authority to issue securities to the public in an amount equal to the March 1996 Social Security benefit payments. Treasury issued about $29 billion of securities on February 23, 1996, and, under P.L. 104-103, these new securities were not to count against the debt limit until March 15, 1996. On March 7, 1996, Congress passed P.L. 104-115, which amended P.L. 104-103 to permit Treasury to continue investing payroll tax revenues in government securities and also to extend the exemption of the securities issued under P.L. 104-103 from counting against the debt limit until March 30, 1996.

The debt limit was permanently increased on March 29, 1996 (P.L. 104-121) from $4,900 billion to $5,500 billion. P.L. 104-121 also codified Congress's understanding that the Secretary of the Treasury and other federal officials are not authorized to use Social Security and Medicare funds for debt management purposes.[94] SSA states the following:

---

[91] GAO, *Debt Ceiling Options*, AIMD-96-20R, December 7, 1995, http://archive.gao.gov/paprpdf1/155750.pdf.

[92] Treasury's Exchange Stabilization Fund buys and sells foreign currency to promote exchange rate stability and counter disorderly conditions in the foreign exchange market.

[93] As described later in this **Appendix**, under normal procedures Treasury pays Social Security benefits from the General Fund and offsets this by redeeming an equivalent amount of the trust funds' holdings of government debt. In order to pay Social Security benefits, and depending on the government's cash position at the time, Treasury may need to issue new public debt to raise the cash needed to pay benefits. Treasury may be unable to issue new public debt, however, because of the debt limit. Social Security benefit payments may be delayed or jeopardized if the Treasury does not have enough cash on hand to pay benefits.

[94] See 42 U.S.C. §1320b-15.

Specifically, the Secretary of the Treasury and other federal officials are required not to delay or otherwise underinvest incoming receipts to the Social Security and Medicare Trust Funds. They are also required not to sell, redeem, or otherwise disinvest securities, obligations, or other assets of these Trust Funds except when necessary to provide for the payment of benefits and administrative expenses of the programs.[95]

These restrictions apply to the Federal Old-Age and Survivors Insurance (OASI) Trust Fund, the Federal Disability Insurance (DI) Trust Fund, the Federal Hospital Insurance (HI) Trust Fund, and the Federal Supplementary Medical Insurance (SMI) Trust Fund.

Selected Actions in 2011

Beginning in January 2011, Treasury again took actions to avoid reaching the debt limit and began notifying Congress of its intentions. On January 6, 2011, Treasury Secretary Geithner sent a letter to Congress stating that Treasury had the ability to delay the date by which the debt limit would be reached by utilizing similar methods used during past crises, including declaring a debt issuance suspension period, if necessary. According to Treasury, these actions could delay the date that the debt limit would be reached by several weeks. However, if the debt limit was not raised after that point, payment of other obligations and benefits would be "discontinued, limited, or adversely affected."[96]

On April 4, 2011, Secretary Geithner issued another letter to Congress stating that the debt limit would be reached no later than May 16, 2011, and the use of extraordinary measures would extend Treasury's ability to meet commitments through July 8, 2011. Beyond these extraordinary measures discussed in the letter and detailed earlier, Treasury stated that it did not have other actions available that year that it could take to find additional authority to issue debt. The letter further stated that the sale of certain financial assets would not be a viable option to avoid increasing the debt limit.[97]

On May 2, 2011, Secretary Geithner issued a third letter to Congress reiterating that the debt limit would be reached no later than May 16, 2011, but that the use of extraordinary measures would extend Treasury's ability to meet commitments through August 2, 2011. The revision in the latter date was a result of stronger than expected tax receipts. Further, Secretary Geithner again stated that not raising the debt limit "would have catastrophic economic impact that would be felt by every American" and that federal payments would be affected.[98] In addition, the letter stated that on Friday, May 6, the issuance of State and Local Government Series (SLGS) Treasury securities would be suspended until further notice.[99]

---

[95] U.S. Social Security Administration, "Program Legislation Enacted in Early 1996," *Social Security Bulletin*, vol. 59, no. 2, Summer 1996, p. 65, at http://www.ssa.gov/policy/docs/ssb/v59n2/index html.

[96] Treasury January 6th letter.

[97] Letter from Timothy F. Geithner, Secretary of the Treasury, to the Hon. Harry Reid, Senate Majority Leader, April 4, 2011, available at http://www.treasury.gov/connect/blog/Documents/FINAL%20Letter%2004-04-2011%20Reid%20Debt%20Limit.pdf.

[98] Treasury May 2nd letter.

[99] For more information, see CRS Report R41811, *State and Local Government Series (SLGS) Treasury Debt: A Description*, by Steven Maguire.

On May 16, 2011, Secretary Geithner notified Congress of a debt issuance suspension period and informed them of his intent to utilize extraordinary measures to create additional room under the debt ceiling to allow Treasury to continue funding the operations of the government.[100] Between May 16, 2011, and August 2, 2011, Treasury prematurely redeemed securities of the Civil Service Retirement and Disability Trust Fund and did not invest receipts of the Civil Service Retirement and Disability Trust Fund and the Postal Service Retiree Health Benefit Fund. Treasury also suspended investments in the Exchange Stabilization Fund and the Government Securities Investment Fund (G-Fund) of the Federal Thrift Savings Plan. Because these funds are required by law to be made whole once the debt limit is increased, these specific actions did not affect federal retirees or employees once the debt limit was increased.[101] The debt limit was permanently increased on August 2, 2011 (Budget Control Act of 2011 or BCA; P.L. 112-25), from $14,294 billion to $14,694 billion.

The enactment of P.L. 112-25 provided for three separate debt limit increases. The first, as discussed above, permanently increased the debt limit on August 2, 2011. Thereafter, the debt limit was permanently increased on September 21, 2011, from $14,694 billion to $15,194 billion and on January 27, 2012, from $15,194 billion to $16,394 billion.[102] Secretary Geithner has stated that the current debt limit would be reached on December 31, 2012, and the use of extraordinary measures would provide additional headroom under the debt limit until early 2013.[103]

Views on the Debt Limit, Prioritization, and Default During the 2011 Debt Limit Debate

During the debate over the debt limit in 2011, both the Administration and Congress maintained various views on this issue. Members of the Obama Administration stated that default cannot be avoided if the debt limit is not raised, and that the consequences of a federal default would be serious. Treasury Secretary Geithner's letter of January 6, 2011, provided Treasury's views on the "consequences of default by the United States." The letter described, among other things, federal payments that would be "discontinued, limited, or adversely affected."[104] The letter also said a short-term or limited default on legal obligations would cause "catastrophic damage to the economy."[105] Chairman of the White House Council of Economic Advisers Austan Goolsbee elaborated, saying that a default would cause "a worse financial economic crisis than anything we

---

[100] Treasury May 16th letter.

[101] Letter from Richard L. Gregg, Fiscal Assistant Secretary, Department of the Treasury, to the Hon. John A. Boehner, Speaker of the House, August 24, 2011, available at http://www.treasury.gov/initiatives/Documents/ G%20Fund%20Letters.pdf and Letter to the Hon. Harry Reid, Senate Majority Leader, January 27, 2012, available at http://www.treasury.gov/initiatives/Documents/Debt%20Limit%20CSRDF%20Report%20to%20Reid.pdf.

[102] For more information on the provisions providing for the debt limit to be increased under the BCA, see CRS Report R41965, *The Budget Control Act of 2011*, by Bill Heniff Jr., Elizabeth Rybicki, and Shannon M. Mahan. Prior to the third debt limit increase, investments in the Government Securities Investment Fund (G-Fund) of the Federal Thrift Savings Plan were suspended from January 17 to January 27, 2012. The G-Fund was made whole on January 27, 2012. Letter from Timothy F. Geithner, Secretary of the Treasury, to the Hon. Harry Reid, Senate Majority Leader, January 17, 2012, available at http://www.treasury.gov/initiatives/Documents/011712TFGLettertoReid.pdf.

[103] Letter from Timothy F. Geithner, Secretary of the Treasury, to the Hon. Harry Reid, Senate Majority Leader, December 26, 2012, available at http://www.treasury.gov/connect/blog/Documents/ Sec%20Geithner%20LETTER%2012-26-2012%20Debt%20Limit.pdf.

[104] Letter from Timothy F. Geithner, Secretary of the Treasury, to the Hon. Harry Reid, Senate Majority Leader, January 6, 2011, p. 4.

[105] Ibid., pp. 1, 3.

saw in 2008."[106] Secretary Geithner, in his letter to Congress, added, "Default would have prolonged and far-reaching negative consequences on the safe-haven status of Treasuries and the dollar's dominant role in the international financial system, causing further increases in interest rates and reducing the willingness of investors here and around the world to invest in the United States."[107] In a later online posting, Treasury Deputy Secretary Neal Wolin wrote that proposals to prioritize payments on the national debt above other legal obligations would not prevent default and would bring the same economic consequences Secretary Geithner described.[108] Looking forward, Secretary Geithner said in his letter that in addition to addressing the debt limit, President Obama wanted to work with Congress to address the federal government's fiscal position with particular attention to addressing "medium- and long-term fiscal challenges."[109]

Other policy makers have expressed some contrasting perspectives focusing on the need to tie proposals to raise the debt limit to spending cuts, changes in the budget process, or instructions on how to deal with the payment of obligations if the debt limit is reached. For example, Senator Jim DeMint wrote in an op-ed that a vote to raise the debt limit should be opposed "unless Congress first passes a balanced-budget amendment that requires a two-thirds majority to raise taxes."[110]

Legislative proposals related to the potential debt limit crisis began emerging in early 2011. For example, Senator Pat Toomey and Representative Tom McClintock introduced legislation that, in the event of a debt limit crisis, would require Treasury to make payment of principal and interest on debt held by the public a higher priority than all other federal government obligations (S. 163/H.R. 421, 112th Congress). In a letter to Secretary Geithner, Senator Toomey said "This legislation is designed to maintain orderly financial markets by reassuring investors in U.S. Treasury securities that their investments are perfectly safe even in the unlikely event that the debt limit is temporarily reached."[111] Similarly, Senator David Vitter and Representative Dean Heller introduced legislation that would require priority be given to payment of all obligations on the debt held by the public and Social Security benefits in the event that the debt limit is reached (S. 259/H.R. 568, 112th Congress).[112] Representative Marlin Stutzman introduced legislation that would require priority be given to payment of all obligations on the debt held by the public, Social Security benefits, and specified military expenditures in the event that the debt limit is reached (H.R. 728, 112th Congress).[113] As noted earlier, Congress passed and the President signed the Budget Control Act, which addressed the debt limit and several aspects of fiscal policy.

---

[106] ABC News *This Week*, Transcript: White House Adviser Austan Goolsbee, January 2, 2011, at http://abcnews.go.com/ThisWeek/week-transcript-white-house-adviser-austan-goolsbee/story?id=12522822.

[107] Treasury Secretary Geithner letter, January 6, 2011, p. 4.

[108] Neal Wolin, Deputy Secretary of the Treasury, "Treasury: Proposals to 'Prioritize' Payments on U.S. Debt Not Workable; Would Not Prevent Default," January 21, 2011, at http://www.treasury.gov/connect/blog/Pages/Proposals-to-Prioritize-Payments-on-US-Debt-Not-Workable-Would-Not-Prevent-Default.aspx.

[109] Treasury Secretary Geithner letter, January 6, 2011, p. 4.

[110] Senator Jim DeMint, "More Spending is a Threat to America," *Politico*, January 24, 2011, available at http://www.politico.com/news/stories/0111/48020 html.

[111] Senator Pat Toomey, "Senator Toomey Sends Letter to Secretary Geithner on the Debt Limit," press release, February 2, 2011, http://toomey.senate.gov/record.cfm?id=330828&.

[112] Representative Dean Heller was sworn in to the U.S. Senate on May 9, 2011, to fill the seat of former Senator John Ensign who had resigned.

[113] These are examples of legislation introduced as of February 15, 2011. Some of this legislation has been considered as amendments to other legislation and were tabled or withdrawn. Other legislation has been subsequently introduced, however, this is not intended to be a legislative tracking report. Therefore not all bills are included in the list above.

Social Security Trust Fund Cash and Investment Management Practices

By law, the Social Security Trust Funds must be invested in interest-bearing obligations of the United States or in obligations guaranteed as to both principal and interest by the United States (42 U.S.C. §401(d) and 42 U.S.C. §1320b-15).[114] The securities that Treasury issues to the Social Security Trust Funds count toward the federal debt limit.

Under normal procedures, Social Security revenues (Social Security payroll taxes and individual income taxes) are immediately credited to the Social Security Trust Funds in the form of short-term, non-marketable Treasury securities called certificates of indebtedness (CIs). Under the terms of this exchange, when Treasury credits payroll tax and other revenues to Social Security in the form of CIs, the revenues themselves become available in the General Fund for other government operations.

CIs generally mature on the following June 30. Each June 30, any surplus for the year is converted from short-term Treasury securities to long-term, non-marketable Treasury securities called "special-issue obligations" or "specials."[115] In addition, other special issues that have just matured and that are not needed to pay near-term benefits are reinvested in special-issue obligations. Interest income is credited to the trust funds semi-annually (on June 30 and December 31) in the form of additional special-issue obligations.[116]

Social Security benefits are paid by Treasury from the General Fund. When Treasury pays Social Security benefits, it redeems an equivalent amount of Treasury securities held by the trust funds in order to reimburse the General Fund.

The Social Security program is projected to run a cash deficit through the 75-year forecast period. That is, Social Security's tax revenues are projected to be less than outlays for benefit payments and administration.[117] In a year when Social Security runs a cash flow deficit, Treasury redeems some long-term government securities held by the trust funds. However, Social Security will still need to invest in non-marketable, short-term government securities to manage short-term cash flows during the periods between receiving revenues and paying benefits (42 U.S.C. §401(a), 42 U.S.C. §401(d) and 42 U.S.C. §1320b-15). Investing the trust funds' revenues for even very short

---

[114] There are two sources of Social Security revenues: (1) payroll taxes paid by workers and employers and (2) federal income taxes paid by some beneficiaries on a portion of their benefits. In addition, Social Security receives income from trust fund investments. Interest income is paid to the trust funds as a credit from the General Fund to the trust funds, in the form of additional non-marketable government securities.

[115] The trust funds' long-term securities have maturities ranging from 1 to 15 years and normally mature in June of the applicable year.

[116] For a detailed discussion, see Social Security Administration, Office of the Chief Actuary, *Social Security Trust Fund Investment Policies and Practices*, Actuarial Note Number 142, January 1999, http://www.ssa.gov/OACT/NOTES/pdf_notes/note142.pdf (hereinafter cited as SSA Actuarial Note Number 142).

[117] For SSA's projections of Social Security Trust Fund operations, see 2013 Annual Report of the Board of Trustees of the Federal Old-Age and Survivors Insurance and Federal Disability Insurance Trust Funds, Washington, DC, May 31, 2013, http://www.socialsecurity.gov/OACT/TR/2013/tr2013.pdf. Social Security's cash deficit will be offset by interest income for many years, with the result that Social Security will have a positive total trust fund balance until the trust funds are exhausted in 2033 under the intermediate projections of the Social Security Board of Trustees. Social Security benefits scheduled under current law can be paid in full as long as there is a sufficient balance in the trust funds.

periods ensures that the trust funds maximize their interest earnings. Social Security will also need to invest in non-marketable, long-term government securities in June of each year, when short-term and certain long-term trust fund securities mature and amounts not needed to pay near-term benefits are rolled over into long-term government securities, and in June and December of each year, when semi-annual interest income is paid in the form of government securities.

In 2011 and 2012, Social Security drew on general revenues as a result of the Tax Relief, Unemployment Insurance Reauthorization, and Job Creation Act of 2010 (P.L. 111-312, as amended by P.L. 112-78 and P.L. 112-96). P.L. 111-312 provided a temporary 2 percentage point reduction in the Social Security payroll tax for employees and the self-employed in 2011, resulting in a tax rate of 4.2% for employees and 10.4% for the self-employed.[118] To protect the trust funds, P.L. 111-312 appropriated to the Social Security Trust Funds amounts equal to the reduction in payroll tax revenues. P.L. 111-312 specified that the appropriated amounts "shall be transferred from the General Fund at such times and in such manner as to replicate to the extent possible the transfers which would have occurred to such Trust Fund had such amendments not been enacted."[119] On December 23, 2011, Congress passed H.R. 3765 and President Obama signed the bill into law as P.L. 112-78 to extend the payroll tax reduction for workers and the general revenue transfers through February 2012. On February 17, 2012, the House and the Senate agreed to the conference report on H.R. 3630, which further extended the payroll tax reduction for workers and the general revenue transfers through the end of calendar year 2012. H.R. 3630 was signed into law by President Obama on February 22, 2012 (P.L. 112-96).

Depending on the extent and duration of any future debt limit crisis, and also on Treasury prioritization decisions, Social Security Trust Fund investment management procedures and benefit payments potentially could be affected because of the requirement that Treasury obligations cannot be issued to the Social Security Trust Funds if doing so would exceed the debt limit.[120] At the same time, as described above, P.L. 104-121 restricts the Treasury Secretary's ability to delay or otherwise underinvest incoming receipts to the Social Security and Medicare Trust Funds. Delayed issuance of government obligations to the Trust Funds, or early redemption of some Trust Fund assets, could accelerate depletion of the Trust Funds and move up the expected insolvency date, absent congressional action to make the Trust Funds whole.

Depending on the government's cash position in a given month, Treasury may need to issue new public debt to raise the cash needed to pay benefits. Treasury may be unable to issue new public debt, however, if doing so would exceed the debt limit. Social Security benefit payments may be delayed or jeopardized if Treasury does not have enough cash on hand to pay benefits.

---

[118] P.L. 111-312, as amended by P.L. 112-78 and P.L. 112-96, made no change to the Social Security payroll tax rate for employers (6.2%) or to the amount of wages and net self-employment income subject to the Social Security payroll tax ($113,700 in 2013).

[119] See P.L. 111-312, Title VI (Temporary Employee Payroll Tax Cut), at http://www.gpo.gov/fdsys/pkg/PLAW-111publ312/pdf/PLAW-111publ312.pdf.

[120] SSA Actuarial Note Number 142, p. 3.

Author Contact Information

Mindy R. Levit, Coordinator
Specialist in Public Finance
mlevit@crs.loc.gov, 7-7792

Clinton T. Brass
Specialist in Government Organization and
Management
cbrass@crs.loc.gov, 7-4536

Thomas J. Nicola
Legislative Attorney
tnicola@crs.loc.gov, 7-5004

Dawn Nuschler
Specialist in Income Security
dnuschler@crs.loc.gov, 7-6283

Acknowledgments

The authors wish to thank D. Andrew Austin and Marc Labonte for their helpful comments on this report and former CRS analyst Alison M. Shelton for her contributions to this report.